SPELLbinding

ꕥ Other Hay House Titles ꕥ
of Related Interest

All of the above are available at your local bookstore,
or may be ordered through Hay House, Inc.:

(800) 654-5126 or **(760) 431-7695**
(800) 650-5115 (fax) or **(760) 431-6948 (fax)**
www.hayhouse.com

SPELLbinding

Claudia Blaxell

**Spells and Rituals
That Will Empower
Your Life**

Hay House, Inc.
Carlsbad, California • Sydney, Australia

Published and distributed in the United States by: Hay House, Inc., P.O. Box 5100, Carlsbad, CA 92018-5100 • (800) 654-5126 • (800) 650-5115 (fax) www.hayhouse.com

Editorial supervision: Jill Kramer • *Design:* Charles McStravick

Library of Congress Cataloging-in-Publication Data

Blaxell, Claudia.
    Spellbinding: spells and rituals that will empower your life / Claudia Blaxell
    p. cm.
    Includes biographical references (p.).
    ISBN 1-56170-869-0 (tradepaper)
    1. Magic. 2. Charms. I. Title.

    BF1611 .B57 2001
    133.4.4—dc21

                                    2001016924

                        ISBN 1-56170-869-0

            04 03 02 01   4 3 2 1
                1st printing, November 2001

                    Printed in Canada

๑ Contents ๑

PART I: Creating a Magical Life

PART II: Spells

PART I

Creating a
Magical Life

CHAPTER ONE

What Is Magic?

Magic is the practice of influencing energy to achieve a goal or to make a dream come true. The energy that courses through your body is the same energy that permeates nature and the entire Universe, so it is within your power to harness and shape this energy to bring about the changes you desire. Magic doesn't require special gifts or supernatural powers; but to work powerful magic, you need to be in tune with the laws of nature, and you must firmly believe that you will achieve your desired end.

Magic has been practiced since the Stone Age. Cave paintings and other archaeological findings from the Paleolithic period show that magical rites were carried out with each changing season. In ancient Mesopotamia, the Sumerians used magic to protect against war and floods, as did the Assyrians and Chaldeans. However, the ancient Egyptians were the first civilization to develop a sophisticated system of magic. Their deep spirituality and profound understanding of the human mind lent great power to their elaborate ceremonies, spells, and burial rites. Egyptian magicians aimed to control the will of the gods and goddesses to create good fortune in the lives and after-lives of those they loved and respected—

or harm to those who dared transgress their laws and religious beliefs.

According to popular legend, Lord Carnarvon, the first man to enter King Tutankhamen's tomb upon its discovery in 1922, died hours later from a poisonous insect bite. The death has since been connected to a curse inscribed on the tomb's walls. Another famous curse has been linked to a mummy containing the body of a priestess who was a devotee of the Egyptian god Ra: A few days after it was purchased from the Egyptian government in 1881, its English custodian, Douglas Murray, committed suicide on his way home with it. After the mummy was accepted by the British museum, one of the two men who carried it in died the next day, and the photographer employed to photograph it died immediately after taking the photo. Subsequently, the mummy found itself in the hands of an American entrepreneur, but it never arrived in the United States . . . as the ship on which it traveled was the SS *Titanic*.

Over the centuries, the principles of magic have spread to the Middle East, Greece, Rome, Russia, India, Tibet, the Americas, Africa, Australia, and Polynesia. The Hebrew Kabbalah, which drew much of its inspiration from the Egyptians, has greatly influenced modern occultism, particularly the "high" or ceremonial magic developed by the Hermetic Order of the Golden Dawn. This talented group of mystical seekers—among them the eminent authority on Western magic, Dr. Israel Regardie; the occult scholar Arthur E. Waite; and the eccentric ritual magician, Aleister Crowley—worked with ten spheres of consciousness called "the sephiroth," represented symbolically on the Kabbalah's Tree of Life. Each sphere was associated with a different aspect of the human psyche and specific gods and goddesses. Through complex ceremonial procedures, invocations, and visualizations, the Golden Dawn magicians aimed to reach a sublime level of spiritual transcendence in order to implement their magical powers.

Modern witchcraft or folk magic has its roots in paganism, the "Old Religion" that prevailed in Western Europe before Christianity. The Old Religion was a way of life rather than a doctrine, as it was based on a love and respect for nature. Plants, animals, stars and planets were thought to have a magical consciousness. Followers of the Old Religion structured their lives around the cycle of the seasons and the monthly phases of the moon. They worshiped various forms of the goddess, the great mother of the earth and Universe, and recognized her essence in all living things.

As bearers of life, women were seen as having an innate connection to the earth in the pre-Christian era, and were revered in society for their ability to work magic for healing, growth, and change. Up until the 12th century—when witch hunting began in Europe—women roamed meadows and woodlands by the waxing and waning of the moon, gathering herbs and other magical ingredients for their spells and remedies.

These wise women and healers are believed to have had acute psychic powers and the ability to change energy into matter—and matter into energy—at will. In recent years, the secret arts of what has become known as "witchcraft" have become a subject of intrigue as more people seek to reclaim their power.

ॐ ॐ ॐ

CHAPTER TWO

How Do Spells Work?

Spells are an effective way of projecting your will and intention into the Universe to create the change you desire. Most spells involve the use of natural ingredients such as crystals, herbs, and incense, as well as objects such as photographs or anything that has been in contact with the person you wish to influence. These items are an integral part of spell casting, as they serve to connect the willpower of the magician with the energy of the Universe. However, the most fundamental catalyst for a successful spell is thought.

Magic is based on the idea that the events that take place in the physical world are just one aspect of reality—that is, what we perceive with our five senses are simply the external manifestations of deeper processes at work. The human mind has many levels of awareness: On a conscious level, it takes things at face value and discerns meaning; and on an unconscious level, it's capable of picking up on people's thoughts and transmitting them to others. While this may sound peculiar, it's actually quite simple.

Recent advances in quantum physics have shown that thoughts are energy, and like electrical impulses, they jump. For this reason, at any given moment, your thoughts are affecting the people around you as well as shaping your life. Most of the time, we don't attempt to control our thoughts; therefore, they jump from one subject to another in a random, rapid-fire way, which at times makes our lives seem chaotic. Spells allow you to concentrate and direct your thought energy toward a specific goal or purpose. When your intention is clear and your thoughts are charged with passion and determination, you instantly ascend to a level of awareness where you can create whatever it is that you desire. This level of awareness is known as the *universal energy field*, a domain where the unconscious minds and mental processes of all human beings are linked. By tapping in to the universal energy field when you cast a spell, it's possible to influence a person's thought processes on an unconscious level and affect their behavior accordingly. Like making a call on a cell phone, you simply attune to the person you wish to contact, leave your message, and then wait for them to accept it. If this is hard for you to conceptualize, think of it like this: A cell phone is just a silicon chip, a piece of plastic, a battery, and an antenna—it's very crude compared to the human brain—yet it's capable of transmitting your voice, thoughts, and feelings across continents without any connecting wires or attachments. So, imagine what your brain can do!

⑤ ⑤ ⑤

CHAPTER THREE

The Laws of Magic

There are no set rules for casting spells, but there are two laws of magic that are worth remembering. First, what you send out will come back to you threefold, so if you feel inclined to use magic for the purpose of making someone else feel uncomfortable, do so at your own risk. Second, your spell is less likely to work if you tell everyone about it. If you keep it a secret, you won't be influenced by anyone else's opinion, which may weaken the energy of your spell.

Spell casting is highly personal. The spells in this book have been chosen for their speed and effectiveness, but they will only come to life if you infuse them with your intent, passion, and creativity. When casting a spell, follow your intuition, and don't be afraid to add extra ingredients if you feel it will help. Remember, the more you engage the force of your personality, the more successful your spell will be.

𝕾 𝕾 𝕾

CHAPTER FOUR

Magical Tools

Magical tools are an important part of spell casting, as they help you to connect to your intent. There are many ways to work with your intent to empower a spell, and objects from nature that represent the four elements—earth, air, fire, and water—are important. It's also appropriate to use any personal possessions that hold special meaning for you. Following are some suggestions.

Plants

Every plant has an energetic field or aura that has a subtle effect on people, animals, and the surrounding environment. When using flowers, herbs, or fruit in spells, try to match their energetic properties (earth, air, fire, or water) with the purpose of your spell.

Spell	Plants	Element
Communication, Speed, Friendship, Clarity, Protection Dispelling Negativity	Fenugreek, Fennel, Lavender, Marjoram, Valerian	Air
Love, Pleasure, Growth, Sensuality, Prosperity, Fertility, Health, Discipline	Elderflower, Apple, Rose, Pennyroyal, Clove, Yarrow, Vervain	Earth
Action, Passion, Sexual Union, Marriage, Courage, Determination	Basil, Cinnamon, Pepper, Nettle, Rosemary, Chili, Passionflower	Fire
Psychic Ability, Creativity, Intuition, Healing, Protection, Romance, Dreams	Mugwort, Iris, Willow, Lily, Seaweed, Cucumber	Water

Candles

Candles are associated with the element fire. They help to focus concentration and communication, and add ambience to a room. Before you light a candle, it's a good idea to charge it with your energy. You can also inscribe it with names and symbols, or anoint it with essential oils to enhance its magical purpose. As the flame burns, it will project your intention out into the Universe. The color of a candle is important, too. Red candles, for instance, promote courage, vitality, and sexual expression, while pink candles are ideal for love and romance. Green candles are good for enhancing growth and creativity. Purple candles are used to attract luck and wealth. Blue candles enhance health, intuition, and psychological balance. Black candles absorb and dispel negative energy. White candles promote protection and purification.

Incense

Incense is associated with the element air and has a purifying effect on the energy of a room. It's one of the most powerful tools of magic because its scent can help to center you and direct focus on your intent. It also stimulates imagination and helps you to become a clear channel for the reception and projection of energy by diverting your attention away from distracting thoughts and emotions.

Wand

The wand is associated with the element fire, and is used to direct will and intention to a designated place or person to engender change. The wand you use can be a household object, such as a wooden spoon or broomstick, or you can make a wand yourself from a tree branch. Remove any leaves from the branch, and then whittle the end to a point. For greater effectiveness, you may wish to attach a crystal to the end of your wand. Simply chop off the tip, gouge a small hollow into the wood, insert the crystal, and secure it with leather or hemp thread.

Pentacle

The pentacle, or five-pointed star, is aligned with the element earth, and is usually made from metal or wood. It's worn on the body or used in magic for protection against negative or undesirable influences. Contrary to popular belief, the pentacle is not a Satanic symbol, but a symbol of life. Its five points represent the five senses—as well as air, earth, fire, water, and spirit, which are the five components of magical power.

Chalice

Associated with the element *water*, the chalice is a magical cup, often painted or engraved with vines and fruit. It's filled with wine and offered to the god and/or goddess during magical rites. If you prefer, you can fill your chalice with spring water, magic dust, or a potion.

Crystals

Crystals are used in magic to direct energy. Different crystals emit different electromagnetic vibrations that can be utilized for healing, protection, fertility, good fortune, clarity, focus, courage, psychic ability, attracting love, and repelling negativity.

ᛋ **Amethyst:** Ruled by Jupiter and Neptune and aligned with *water*, amethyst brings about peace, clarity, emotional balance, and enhanced psychic awareness. It's used in spells to banish doubt and despondency. It can also help to remove obstacles that may stand in the way of your intended desires, and can strengthen bonds of love.

ᛋ **Aventurine:** Ruled by Mercury and aligned with *air*, aventurine engenders creativity, healing, and luck, and increases mental acuity.

It's used in spells to draw money to you quickly.

Ⓢ **Carnelian:** Ruled by the sun and aligned with fire, carnelian strengthens courage, confidence, and sexual expression. It's an uplifting stone that helps to conquer fear and negative thoughts. It's used to project energy in love spells.

Ⓢ **Clear Quartz:** Ruled by the sun and moon and aligned with fire and water, clear quartz is an all-around power crystal that awakens the unconscious mind. It magnifies the effectiveness of any spell; and has protective, healing qualities.

Ⓢ **Emerald:** Ruled by Venus and aligned with earth, emerald is utilized in spells for manifesting love and material abundance. It also dispels evil and enhances psychic ability.

§ **Green Calcite:** Ruled by Venus and aligned with earth, green calcite is a healing stone. It's also used in spells to attract wealth and prosperity.

§ **Hematite:** Ruled by Saturn and aligned with fire, hematite helps to ground your intention. It's used in healing rituals and spells for manifesting power.

§ **Jade:** Ruled by Venus and aligned with water, jade is a soothing, cooling stone that promotes health, longevity, and prosperity. In China, it's traditionally given to the bride by the groom to ensure fidelity in marriage. It's used in spells to attract love.

§ **Jet:** Ruled by Saturn and aligned with earth, jet is ancient, fossilized wood that promotes health, luck, and protection. It has the ability to absorb negativity and empower the psychic mind.

🌀 **Lapis Lazuli:** Ruled by Venus and aligned with *water*, lapis lazuli is a healing, revitalizing stone that increases psychic awareness. It's used in spells to enhance love, health, and courage.

🌀 **Malachite:** Ruled by Venus and aligned with *earth*, malachite cools fiery emotions and protects against hostility. It's used in all types of spells to energize and expand the power of your intent.

🌀 **Moonstone:** Ruled by the moon and aligned with *water*, moonstone has a loving vibration and helps to stimulate psychic ability. In spells, it's used to tap in to the feelings of estranged loved ones.

🌀 **Rose Quartz:** Ruled by the moon and Venus and aligned with the element of *water*, rose quartz is a calming, soothing stone that promotes peace, relaxation, and harmonious interactions with others. It's used in spells to draw love, or to intensify an existing relationship.

- **Tiger's Eye:** Ruled by the sun and aligned with fire, tiger's eye is an energizing stone that attracts luck and money. It's also useful for calming the overactivity of the conscious mind, helping to strengthen your will and intent.

- **Turquoise:** Ruled by Venus and Neptune and aligned with earth, turquoise is the ideal stone for ensuring good fortune when traveling. It promotes courage and joy, and protects against physical danger. It also draws friendship and beauty to you.

Altar

An altar is a sacred surface where you can keep your magical tools. You might like to use a special table or dresser as your altar, but if you have limited room, the top of a bookcase or chest of drawers will do. It's important to clean your altar regularly to keep it free of dust and ash. Consecrate it by tracing your wand around the perimeter in a clockwise direction, saying,

You are now a magnet
for positive and creative energy.
I call upon the guardians of the north,
south, east, and west to protect you from
negativity and harmful energy.

Personal Objects

The use of personal objects adds your individual touch to a spell. An object that has been taken from somebody else is said to work "empathically" with that person, as it creates a connection to them. Examples include a lock of hair, a piece of clothing or jewelry, or just about anything the person comes into contact with on a regular basis. Photographs and talismans can also be used in spells to help focus your own energy.

🌀 🌀 🌀

CHAPTER FIVE

Your Magical Environment

B efore you begin a spell, it's important to create a sacred space that will support your purpose.

Cleansing and purifying is best done at sunset, the time of release. Make sure the room you choose to perform your spells in is tidy and dust free. Throw out any junk you have accumulated, and don't leave dirty clothes or dishes lying around, as they will interfere with the energy of the present moment and block the power of your intention. Open the windows and doors; and let clean, fresh air and energy flow into the room. When you've finished cleaning, perform a quick purification ritual.

Purification Ritual

Light two black candles and place them on either side of your altar. Burn some frank-incense incense, and disperse the smoke around the room in a clockwise direction, saying,

> May the elements of air and
> fire purify this room.
> Negative energy begone.

Now, close the windows and doors, snuff out the candle flames, and know that you have banished all bad vibes.

෪ ෪ ෪

CHAPTER SIX

Preparing the Body and Mind for Magic

Your magical power will be greatly enhanced if you take time to bond with nature. Walking through the trees or swimming in the ocean are perfect ways to purify your body and remove any unwanted energy you may have attracted during the day. If you feel irritable, anxious, vague, or confused, it's a good idea to spend as much time as you can near water to gain clarity on the issue that is bothering you. If you don't live near water, you can always relax in a bath.

Ritual Bath

Run yourself a warm bath, and once it's full, add a couple of drops of lavender and juniper oil to drive out negative feelings and stimulate focus. If you like, you can also include any herbs or oils you plan to use in your spell. Light some candles, lower your body into the water, lie back, and relax. Stretch your muscles to release any tension; and take ten slow, deep breaths. When you feel calm and centered, close your eyes and visualize the intent of your spell—and its subsequent success. Lose yourself in the visualization, and feel the satisfaction and pleasure it brings. As your energy moves toward your intent, say,

With the element of water,
I wash myself clean,
To remove any obstacles
that remain unseen.
As I leave the past behind,
I awaken the powers of my psychic mind.

When you're ready, dry yourself with a clean towel and get dressed in some comfortable clothing, or, if you prefer, remain naked.

Casting spells or performing magical rites while naked (or "sky-clad") is an ancient practice that dates back to the pre-Christian era. Followers of the Old Religion celebrated the cycles of the earth and the night of the full moon naked.

The idea behind being sky-clad is that energy can flow more freely from your body when it's not clothed, as there is no barrier between you and the Universe. If performing spells naked allows you to be truly free, it will empower your spells.

ꥃ ꥃ ꥃ

CHAPTER SEVEN

Masculine and Feminine Energy

Spells involve action and intuitive thought, and they require the integration of feminine "receptive" energy and masculine "projective" energy. For centuries, humans have recognized that the union of masculine and feminine energy is fundamental to the creation of matter. In Babylon, it was believed that the union of Ishtar and Tammuz created Earth. Similarly, in Egypt, it was the union of Isis and Osiris that resulted in the birth of Horus, who became king of the gods.

The Chinese also recognize the dynamic and creative interplay between the female and male energies—yin and yang—which are thought to exist in all living things. Every person, regardless of his or her physical gender, has a strong side, a weak side, a dark side, a sunny side, a good side, a bad side, and a contrasexual side. Psychotherapist Carl Jung referred to the feminine aspect as *anima*, and the masculine aspect as *animus*. For your spells to be successful, it's important to exercise both these fundamental polarities so you can fully express your creative power. Try to avoid the tendency to bury and neglect your contrasexual nature by conforming to sex-role stereotypes. Crazy societal ideals of "real" men and women only serve to squelch your individuality.

If you're female, your animus can lend great force and vitality to a spell. It arouses strength and independence, and enables you to act on your inner wisdom—it's the practical energy that brings your intent to manifestation. If you're male, your anima lends focus and emotional depth to a spell. It strengthens your connection to your inner world, and increases awareness of your thoughts and feelings—it's the creative energy that allows your intuitive power to unfold.

The more you explore and nurture your contrasexual nature, the easier you'll find it to bridge the gap between spirit and matter, and the more effective your spells will be.

Ⓢ Ⓢ Ⓢ

CHAPTER EIGHT

Instincts and Emotions

The most effective spells are those that are driven by your instincts and emotions. Anger, joy, rage, resentment, rapture, love, ecstasy, sadness, courage, and determination are all products of your personal power, and they provide you with the impetus to bring your desires to manifestation. If your spell doesn't come from the heart, your magic won't work, so it's important that you honor your true feelings before you cast one. Let whatever comes up, come up—even your darkest thoughts and emotions. In our society, which often devalues anything that isn't rational, predictable, and within the power of human control, it's easy to feel removed from your emotions. You may feel compelled to deny or repress feelings such as pain, rage, and resentment for fear of seeing a side of yourself that you're not comfortable with. But it's important to realize that the more you try to turn your back on your shadow side, the more overwhelming it becomes. Recognizing and accepting your shadow not only frees you from its grip, but it allows you to tap in to your intuition, which lends a great deal of power to a spell. So the next time you're feeling angry or irritable, know that you're a wild and beautiful creature who is capable of initiating a new cycle in your life.

Spells should be approached with a sense of determination and optimism. You must know that you'll create whatever it is you desire. To increase your psychic sensitivity, anoint your third-eye area (in between and just above your eyebrows) with your favorite essential oil. A blend of patchouli, jasmine, and cedarwood will help to ground you and build confidence. As you visualize and project your intent, random thoughts may arise in your mind; accept them and then let them go. Take your time and feel your body resonate with the energy of the Universe. Eventually, the chatter of your conscious mind will cease, and you'll become a clear channel of focused thought and vibration. When your intention is fixed and intense, begin your spell.

Ⓢ Ⓢ Ⓢ

CHAPTER NINE

The Magic Circle

Most spells are best performed within a magic circle, which can be drawn on a large piece of fabric or marked out with crystals or stones. Circles have long been used for magical work, the earliest evidence documented in ancient Assyria. With no end and no beginning, the circle serves to protect you against negative external energy, and helps to intensify the magical energy that is generated within.

Arrange the objects you intend to use in your spell inside your magic circle. It's appropriate to place candles at the four cardinal points—north, south, east, and west—for added protection and power. Stand in the center of the circle, and spend a few moments in silence, taking a few deep breaths. Then with your wand, trace the circle's circumference in a clockwise direction, saying,

I cast this circle to keep out harmful forces,
and draw in only positive energy
that will enhance my spell.
So be it.

Then invite in the guardians of the directions. These ethereal beings guard the circle and raise its energy. They also help to initiate change and manifestation. As you light each candle at the four cardinal points, say,

Guardians of the north,
south, east, and west, be here now.
Protect me well and speed my spell.

As the energy begins to rise, sit down comfortably in the center of the circle and call in the gods and goddesses you wish to assist you in your spell. The deities you choose should reflect the nature of your spell. For example, if you were casting a love spell, you would invoke a goddess of love and fertility such as Aphrodite, Venus, or Ishtar, as well as, perhaps, a god such as Cernunnos or Ra to instigate action and change. If you have a special affinity with a particular deity, you may wish to have him/her by your side during every spell (see below for more information). Once you've called in your gods and goddesses, say,

Gracious god and/or goddess
[call them by name],
send me your power.
Bring me my goal
in the perfect hour.

Once your spell is complete, thank the god and/or goddess for their assistance, and release the guardians of the directions by blowing out each candle. Then open the circle by tracing around its perimeter with your wand in a counterclockwise direction, saying,

The circle is open but not unbroken.

With that, the energy of the circle moves into the Universe to do its work.

§ § §

CHAPTER TEN

Invoking the Gods and Goddesses

Throughout history, humankind has worshiped various gods and goddesses, each of whom governs a specific aspect of nature, or human behavior and emotion. These divine beings are not real in a physical sense, but are mythological representations of ourselves, which manifest as energy through time, space, and all living things.

When you invoke a particular deity, you connect with their unique qualities and powers to bring about change. Each god and goddess serves to activate the wisdom of your innermost self so that you can find creative solutions to the challenges of life.

Goddesses

- ⑨ **Aphrodite (Greek):** Goddess of love and beauty. Aphrodite enhances beauty and confidence, and inspires people to fall in love. Invoke her to create an intense and passionate union between you and your lover.

- ⑨ **Brigit (Celtic):** Goddess of the hearth. Brigit can be invoked when doing spells for the home and household. She helps to nourish domestic relationships and raise the energy of your home environment.

- ⑨ **Cerridwen (Welsh):** Goddess of wisdom and inspiration. Call on Cerridwen to assist you with study or painstaking work. She'll give you the knowledge and commitment you need to achieve your long-term goals.

ॐ **Demeter (Greek):** Goddess of the harvest and fertility. This practical and nurturing mother figure guards all aspects of conception, birth, and life. She'll ensure that any endeavor you undertake has a fruitful result.

ॐ **Diana (Roman):** Goddess of the hunt and moon. Diana is an independent, free-spirited maiden who listens to the wisdom of instinct. She'll give you the courage and confidence to take risks in career and relationships.

ॐ **Epona (Celtic):** Goddess of fertility, war, and sovereignty. This maternal warrior has a strong procreative drive. She'll help you take control of your life and ensure that your plans are fully executed.

ॐ **Ishtar (Babylonian):** Goddess of love, fertility, sovereignty, and the underworld. Ishtar will help you fulfill your emotional needs and heighten your sexual prowess. Ask her for assistance when venturing into darkness or the unknown.

§ **Isis (Egyptian):** "Great Mother of All." Isis is a goddess of healing, magic, wisdom, love, and fertility. Call on her to enhance the power of any spell—she'll remove any obstacle that blocks your progress.

§ **Kali (Hindu):** Goddess of destruction and creation. Often called "The Black Mother," Kali is the feared but necessary destroyer of things that don't serve us. Invoke her when doing spells to restore order and balance in your life after chaos has struck.

§ **Morgain (Celtic):** Goddess of wisdom and sovereignty. Morgain is a wise and powerful matriarch who always knows the correct path of action. Call on her when

making an important decision—
she'll help you realize your own
power.

🆂 **Scathach: (Celtic):** Goddess of
war. This wild warrior woman will
give you strength during times of
upheaval, as well as the motivation
and confidence to move on in life.
Invoke her when doing protection
spells.

Gods

🆂 **Apollo (Greek):** God of the sun.
This zealous and passionate god
embodies the qualities of wisdom
and spirituality. He can help you
enhance powers of creativity and
bring forth new beginnings.

🆂 **Dionysus (Greek):** God of festivity
and fertility. Dionysus will bring
fun, joy, and pleasure into your

life. Call on him when you wish to seek gratification.

§ **Cernunnos (Celtic):** God of the wild things. This ancient horned god is the original ruler of the animals and forests. Invoke him to liberate your untamed, instinctive nature—he'll help give you a freer and more confident approach to sex and relationships.

§ **Mercury (Roman):** God of communication. Lively, versatile, and fast-acting, Mercury will ensure that any message you wish to convey is transferred swiftly. He'll also instigate movement in affairs that are fraught with obstacles, or where communication is blocked.

§ **Merlin (Celtic):** God of wisdom and magic. This skillful magician will greatly enhance the effectiveness of any spell. Invoke him to help bring your intent to manifestation.

ᔕ **Osiris (Egyptian):** God of death, rebirth, and fertility. Call on Osiris when you want to end a problematic situation and initiate a new beginning, for he'll give you the wisdom, strength, and unwavering confidence you need to achieve your intent.

ᔕ **Pan (Greek):** God of the forest and earth. This restless, promiscuous, free-spirited god will bring you many new sexual experiences. Invoke him when you need to let go of rigid thoughts and behavior patterns, or if you simply want to have some fun!

ᔕ **Pluto (Roman):** God of the underworld. Pluto will help you probe deep into the reaches of your inner world and connect with your feelings. Invoke him when you need to transform dark thoughts, or resolve an issue that's troubling you.

§ **Ra (Egyptian):** God of the sun. Call on this benevolent and illuminating god when you want to cultivate a new project or relationship—he can help lift a black cloud of depression and bring fulfillment to many areas of your life.

§ **Vishnu (Hindu):** God of the sun and fertility. Vishnu can assist you with the creative process and will help bring about clarity when you're feeling confused, instill order when your life is in turmoil, and create abundance when your bank account is barren.

§ **Zeus (Greek):** God of the sky. Zeus will endow you with the qualities of leadership, confidence, and command. Invoke him during spells where strong, decisive action is required.

§ § §

CHAPTER ELEVEN

The Right Time to Prepare Your Spells

There are appropriate days and times of the month for performing certain spells. The success of your spell depends greatly on the phase of the moon. When the moon is waxing (moving toward fullness), it's best to cast spells that relate to beginnings and growth—spells to create a new situation, or nurture and enhance an existing situation. When the moon is waning (fading toward disappearance), it's best to cast spells for protection and elimination— spells to remove blocks and obstacles, or to neutralize problems and harmful energy.

The most powerful time to initiate something new is when the moon first appears as a slender crescent. Bringing a matter to completion is best done just before the moon is full. And the waning moon is the most auspicious time to banish problems and obstacles.

Another thing to consider with regard to appropriate timing is the influence that planetary transits have on spells. When Mercury is in retrograde or backward motion, you should avoid doing spells or rituals of any kind, as this is a time when communication does not flow smoothly and obstacles increase. Lunar eclipses are also problematic for spells, because although they instigate movement and change, their immediate effects are unsettling, and our perceptions are often confused.

There are seven major planetary aspects—conjunction, sextile, semi-sextile, square, trine, quincunx, and opposition—which describe the way two or more planets affect each other in the zodiacal circle. The following aspects produce the best results for spells.

§ When the moon and Mercury are sextile, trine, or semi-sextile, you'll be able to **communicate** your message and intention swiftly and effectively.

§ When the moon and Venus are conjunct, sextile, trine, or semi-sextile, it's a good time to perform **love** spells, as you'll feel loved and loving and will be able to express your emotions with charm and sensitivity.

§ Beneficial aspects between the moon and Mars (sextile, trine, or semi-sextile) will give you the **energy** you need to forcefully propel your spell into action.

§ When the moon and Jupiter combine in easy aspect (sextile, trine, or semi-sextile), your spells will be blessed with **good fortune**. These are particularly auspicious times to cast spells for abundance, success, and expansion.

⑤ Beneficial aspects between the moon and Saturn (sextile, trine, or semi-sextile) will give you a **practical and serious** approach to spells. (But when the aspect between the moon and Saturn is difficult [conjunct, square, opposition, or quincunx], you should avoid spells altogether, as your emotions will be blocked and difficult to express.)

⑤ When the moon and Uranus combine in easy aspect (sextile, trine, or semi-sextile), it's a good time to cast a **bizarre or unusual** spell, as it will be projected passionately at this time.

⑤ You'll feel highly attuned psychically when the moon and Neptune combine in easy aspect (sextile, trine, or semi-sextile). This is advantageous for any type of spell, particularly those relating to **spiritual or artistic** pursuits.

꩜ Beneficial aspects between the
moon and Pluto (sextile, trine,
and semi-sextile) will give you
the strength, determination, and
courage you need for effective
spell casting. These aspects are
especially auspicious for spells
that evoke **deep transformation.**

To stay informed about the phases of the
moon and the movement of the planets,
consult an astrological calender or ephemeris
(an astronomical almanac). These can be
obtained from most esoteric bookstores.

Days

Monday
- Associated with the moon.
- Good for spells that bring about union, and also those that involve the home, family, and domestic front.

Tuesday
- Associated with Mars.
- Good for spells that require a fighting spirit and the will to win, and also those that necessitate fast action.

Wednesday
- Associated with Mercury.
- Good for transmitting messages quickly and concisely, and for spells that involve verbal communication.

Thursday
- Associated with Jupiter.
- Good for attracting material wealth, success, and good fortune.

Friday

- Associated with Venus.
- Good for love spells; and those that bring about friendship, romance, and pleasure.

Saturday

- Associated with Saturn.
- Good for removing obstacles and difficulties from your life.

Sunday

- Associated with the sun.
- Good for spells that enhance your personal power and push you in a new direction.

🌀 🌀 🌀

Spells

PART II

CHAPTER TWELVE

Love and Relationships

Spell to Bewitch Another

Time:

🌀 Perform this spell on a Friday or Sunday, just before the full moon.

You Will Need:

🌀 1 pink candle

🌀 1 dried rose

🌀 1 red ribbon (20 inches)

🌀 Jasmine oil

ى Strong visualization powers

ى Confidence in your ability to spin a
web of intrigue

Action:

Charge the candle, rose, and ribbon with your energy, and anoint the candle with jasmine oil. With the ribbon, tie the rose to the middle of the candle and set it down on the floor. Then light the candle and sit in front of it as it burns.

Close your eyes and draw the goddess Aphrodite to you. Feel the power of her love, beauty, and creativity illuminating your entire being. Think about what an amazing person you are, and the dramatic impact your presence has on a room full of people. Now, in your mind's eye, see your intended lover fall under the spell of your charm. For several minutes, picture the fascination in his/her eyes, and recognize the beauty that he/she sees in you. Then say,

You are under my spell and beginning to see
That now you will not stop thinking of me.
So be it.

Allow the candle flame to burn the rose and ribbon. Gather the remaining ash and place it in the chalice on your altar. Leave it there until your intent is fulfilled.

Spell to Bring Love
into Your Life

Time:

§ Perform this spell on a Thursday or Friday,
when the moon is new.

You Will Need:

§ A heart-shaped box

§ Pink felt (6" x 6")

§ A pair of scissors

§ A needle and thread

§ Glue

§ 1 rose

§ 3 small polished crystals: carnelian,
malachite, and rose quartz

§ 2 fresh basil leaves

§ 4 cloves

§ An infusion of elderflower

§ 3 pink candles

§ 3 black candles

§ Any personal object that suggests love, sex, or intimacy

§ A firm belief that you will attract the person who is meant for you

Action:

Arrange the spell ingredients in your magic circle and surround them with the three black candles. Light the candles, and use the incense to circle the objects in a clockwise direction, saying,

> I banish any harmful energy
> you may contain.

Blow out the black candles and put them aside; then replace them with pink candles. Use the felt to cut out two hearts—sew them together side-by-side. Now glue the hearts to the base of your heart-shaped box. Place the objects you have chosen inside the box, charging them with loving energy as you do so. When you've finished, sprinkle the contents with elderflower tea for added love and protection. As you secure the lid, say,

Magic box, bring me love
with a blessing from above.
Isis and Osiris, make love shine,
and bind my partner's path to mine.

Place the box on your altar or keep it in a special place. In accordance with the principles of feng shui, you might like to keep it in the domain of love and relationships, which is the far right-hand corner of your home.

ﬓ　ﬓ　ﬓ

Spell to Make Love Grow

Time:

🕉 Perform this spell on a Monday, Tuesday, or Friday, when the moon is waxing.
First Q.

You Will Need:

🕉 A glass bottle with a lid

🕉 A pair of scissors

🕉 1 Tbsp. sea salt

🕉 1 pink candle

🕉 1 knife

🕉 Love Oil:

> 3 Tbsp. jojoba oil
> 2 drops jasmine oil
> 2 drops patchouli oil
> 1 drop bergamot oil

🕉 A piece of your lover's clothing

🕉 A piece of your clothing

🕉 A cutting of your lover's hair

🌀 A cutting of your hair

🌀 2 cinnamon sticks

🌀 2 tsp. yarrow

🌀 1 Tbsp. honey

🌀 A piece of the sheet that you and your lover sleep on

🌀 Any personal objects that suggest love, sex, and romance

🌀 Passion, love, and devotion

Action:

Cleanse your magic bottle with salt and water, and dry it in the sun. As the sun's warmth and energy penetrates the glass, make the love oil and prepare a tea of cinnamon, yarrow, and honey. Then assemble all your ingredients and cast a circle.

Carve your name and your lover's name into the candle and imbue it with your energy. Light the candle and let it burn. Place the tea, oil, cloth, hair, and other personal objects into the bottle, fasten the lid, and shake well.

As the ingredients blend, send loving thoughts to your partner and feel the energy grow between you. Visualize your bodies together in a passionate wash of ecstasy as you watch the candle burn. When you're satisfied that your mission is complete, place the candle and bottle on your altar, and let the candle burn down completely. Now you can look forward to an intense exchange of love.

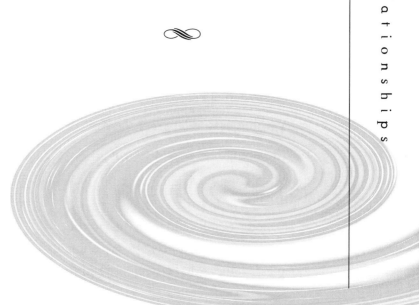

Spell to End a Relationship

Time:

- ᔕ Perform this spell on a Monday or Tuesday, when the moon is waning.
  Last Q.

You Will Need:

- ᔕ 2 black candles
- ᔕ A photo of you and your partner
- ᔕ A pair of scissors
- ᔕ 2 pairs of tweezers
- ᔕ Frankincense incense
- ᔕ 2 Tbsp. lavender
- ᔕ A willingness to let go of the past
- ᔕ The strength to be self-reliant

Action:

Light the candles and burn the incense to neutralize any negative feelings or confused thoughts that may exist between you and your partner. Prepare a lavender tea and sip it slowly throughout the spell. It will help to protect and filter the emotional energy of your psyche.

Sit for a few minutes in quiet meditation and think about all the reasons why your relationship has come to an end. Does your partner drain you of energy? Are your lives moving in different directions? Has your relationship become stale? Do you have communication problems that cannot be resolved? Or have you simply fallen out of love? Allow your true feelings to come to the surface. If you feel anger, grief, guilt, or resentment, acknowledge it and let it go. If you still love your partner, know that it will help you move through this time of transition with sensitivity and understanding.

After you've examined your feelings as honestly as possible, take the photograph of you and your partner and cut it in two so that your images appear on separate halves. Now, with separate tweezers, pick up the images and place them over the candle flames. As each half of the photograph crackles and burns, call the goddess Kali and the god Zeus into the circle to help destroy the bonds that have become limiting. After you've surrendered to the powers of transformation, gather the ashes of the burned photograph and bury them.

Spell to Deter a Love Interest

Time:

🕉 Perform this spell on a Tuesday or Saturday, when the moon is waning.

You Will Need:

🕉 1 tsp. frankincense and myrrh

🕉 ½ tsp. fennel seeds

🕉 ½ tsp. pepper

🕉 ½ tsp. chili powder

🕉 Large charcoal disk

🕉 1 white candle

🕉 1 black candle

🕉 ½ cup sea salt

🕉 A desire to repel, but not harm, the person who won't leave you alone

Action:

Cast a circle, and sprinkle sea salt around its perimeter. Place the black candle to the left of you and the white candle to the right. While lighting the black candle, say, "I neutralize the power of [name of the subject], so they cannot disturb or manipulate me." While lighting the white candle say, "I trust my perceptions and invite only the positive into my life."

Now burn the fennel, pepper, chili, frankincense, and myrrh on the charcoal disk over the flame of the white candle. As the smoke rises and permeates the room, imagine that you're surrounded by a protective shield that can't be penetrated by the person you wish to deter. Visualize their attempts to influence your failure, and finally lose interest. Then say,

The force of your will can't affect me one bit.
I know what I want, and you're not it.
Don't come near me, don't look at me,
don't call me on the phone.
Stay away, stay away, leave me alone.

Leave the herbs to smoulder until the charcoal has completely burned off. Then place the remaining ash in the chalice on your altar. The person who keeps bugging you will stay away.

Spell to Mend a Broken Heart

Time:

ᔕ Perform this spell on a Friday, just before the full moon.

You Will Need:

ᔕ 1 blue candle

ᔕ 1 pink candle

ᔕ 2 drops bergamot oil

ᔕ 2 drops lavender oil

ᔕ 2 drops jasmine oil

ᔕ An infusion of elderflower and yarrow

ᔕ Rose incense

ᔕ 1 silver pentacle

ᔕ 4 large carnelian beads

ᔕ 4 small turquoise beads

ᔕ 4 small amethyst beads

ᔕ Leather cord (1 yard)

Action:

Run yourself a bath. Light the blue candle and place it at the end of the tub. While the bath is filling, make the yarrow and elder-flower tea. When the bath is full, lower yourself into the water and add the berg-amot, lavender, and jasmine oils. As you lie back and relax, slowly sip the tea and bask in the healing energy of the burning blue candle. Notice the uplifting effect that the oils have on your senses, and focus on your beauty and strength. Ask the god Pan and the goddess Diana to join you. They will help you see the past with clarity and accept change. Say,

> *The bonds of the past can serve me no longer.*
> *My heart is mending and growing stronger.*
> *As I release my sorrow and pain,*
> *My heart is free to love again.*

After your bath, dry yourself off and pre-pare for the next part of the spell. Assemble the remaining ingredients, light the incense and pink candle, and sit down comfortably in the center of your circle.

Since prehistoric times, ritual objects such as jewelry, talismans, and mandalas have been used to focus intent. The necklace you are about to make will strengthen your self-confidence and sexual energy, as well as protect you from harmful influences.

Tie a loose knot at one end of the leather cord to prevent the beads from sliding off. Thread one turquoise bead onto the cord, then one amethyst bead, then one carnelian bead, and so on. When you get halfway done, thread the silver pentacle onto the cord so it is positioned in the middle of the necklace. When you've finished, tie two tight knots at either end of the beads to keep them in place. Place the completed necklace around your neck and tie it at the back. You will immediately feel its empowering effects, and your spirits will begin to lift.

Spell to Make Your Lover Call

Time:

§ Perform this spell on a Wednesday or
Friday, when the moon is waxing or
nearly full. *First*

You Will Need:

§ A telephone

§ 2 red candles

§ 2 pink candles

§ A small knife

§ Love Oil:

    3 Tbsp. jojoba oil

    2 drops jasmine oil

    2 drops patchouli oil

    2 drops neroli oil

§ Rose or lotus incense

§ Strong visualization powers

§ Clear, direct communication

Action:

Cast a circle, place the ingredients inside, and light the incense. Carve your name into the pink candles, and your lover's name into the red candles, and anoint them with love oil. Arrange the candles around the telephone, and light them. Then call upon Mercury and Epona to help you inspire your lover to call. Say,

> Set my lover's heart on fire with
> love for me and great desire.
> Stir **[the subject's name's]** feelings
> and make him/her see that
> He/she will have no peace
> until he/she has spoken to me.
> So be it.

Now visualize your lover thinking about you and moving through any communication blocks. See him/her picking up the phone and dialing your number. Feel the mutual excitement as you speak. If your lover has not called within a week, repeat the spell, or call him/her!

CHAPTER THIRTEEN

Money and Work

Spell to Attract Money

Time:

🌀 Perform this spell on a Thursday, when the moon is waxing.

First

You Will Need:

🌀 1 small aventurine crystal

🌀 1 tsp. cinnamon

🌀 1 tsp. cloves

🌀 A mortar and pestle

ॐ ½ cup sea salt

ॐ 1 bowl of water

ॐ A small purple bag

ॐ Inner clarity

ॐ A belief that prosperity is your natural right

Action:

Place the crystal and sea salt into the bowl of water, and leave it under the waxing moon for several days. When the moon is almost full, gather the ingredients together and cast a circle.

Use the mortar and pestle to grind the herbs into a powder. Then hold the crystal in your left hand and concentrate on your financial intent. How much money do you want to have? How will you acquire this money? What will you do with the money once you have it?

When your intention is clear, and you feel satisfied that you have sufficiently charged the crystal and herbs to help bring you the wealth you desire, place them in the purple bag and carry it with you everywhere. Soon your financial success will begin to unfold.

Spell to Manifest
Your Perfect Job or
Business Venture

Time:

Ⓢ Perform this spell on a Tuesday or
Sunday, when the moon is new. *may 6*

You Will Need:

Ⓢ A piece of orange paper (8" x 8")

Ⓢ A pen

Ⓢ Orange ribbon (20")

Ⓢ 2 orange candles

Ⓢ 4 gold coins

Ⓢ 1 small tiger's eye crystal

Ⓢ The strength to trust your heart and
move with it

Action:

Charge the crystal, coins, and candles with your energy, and set them down in front of you. Light the candles and spend a few minutes in quiet meditation thinking about your goal. Write down your ideal job or business venture on the orange paper as clearly and concisely as possible. Wrap the gold coins in the paper, and bind them to the crystal with ribbon. Holding the coins in your left hand, call upon the sun god Ra to help you initiate your new endeavor. Then place the coins between the flaming candles and visualize your intent coming to manifestation. See yourself accomplishing grand tasks in your chosen field, and feel the satisfaction and fulfillment it brings. Now raise the power of your spell by chanting:

My intention is fixed on what I want to do.
I'm about to embark upon something new.
God of the Sun, make my wish come true.
So be it.

Let the candles burn down and out, and place the coins and crystal on your altar. You're now ready to embark on a new career cycle.

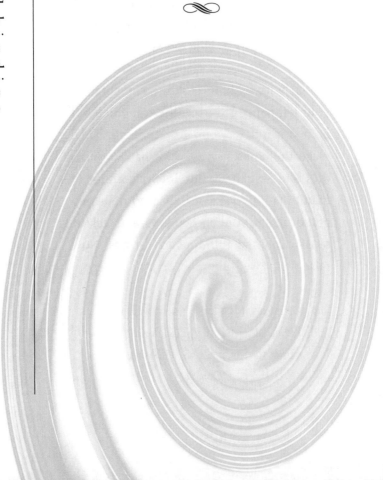

Spell to Ensure Good Fortune in Business

Time:

 Perform this spell on a Thursday, when the moon is waxing.

You Will Need:

 A large glass bowl

 2 jade crystals

 2 tiger's eye crystals

 2 aventurine crystals

 2 malachite crystals

 1 quartz crystal

 9 gold coins

 Symbols of good fortune. (You might like to include a glass, a ceramic or crystal dragon, a lotus flower, or an elephant with a raised trunk.)

⑤   1 bowl of water

⑤   1 Tbsp. sea salt

⑤   4 green candles

⑤   The foresight to recognize opportunity
and make use of it

Action:

Mix the sea salt into the bowl of water
and add the crystals, coins, and symbols.
Leave the bowl under the light of a full moon
for one night. The next day, remove the
objects from the bowl and dry them in the
sun. Your "wealth-attracting" treasure is
now sufficiently cleansed and energized.

Perform the spell in your home, office, or
work environment—wherever your business
is based. Sit down in the center of your magic
circle and set down the glass bowl in front
of you. Place the crystals, coins, and symbols
of good fortune inside the glass bowl, and
position the candles around it at the four
cardinal points (north, south, east, and
west). As you light the candles, say,

*I create this spell to bring finances and good
fortune to my business. Gracious god Mercury,
bestow your gifts of wisdom and communication
upon me so that opportunity
constantly flows to me.*

Blow out the candles and place your
prosperity bowl on your altar or desk—or if
you prefer, you can hide it in a drawer or
cupboard where you keep money or account
books. Once a year, cleanse the contents of
the bowl and repeat the above ritual to
replenish your business with fresh energy.

Spell to Increase Abundance

Time:

§ Perform this spell on a Thursday, when the moon is new.

You Will Need:

§ A small Chinese jade tree

§ A large pot of soil

§ A watering can

§ Natural fertilizer

§ 1 green calcite crystal

§ 2 green candles

§ An awareness of your connection to the earth's creative energy

Action:

Assemble your tools and cast a circle, preferably outdoors. Light the candles and place them around the pot of soil to attract abundance. Now move your hands through the soil and think about all the things you would like your money tree to bring—a blossoming bank account, a house, a business, a trip overseas. Call the goddess Demeter into your circle, and feel her bountiful energy and nurturing touch. Now plant the tree, and as you do, say,

> The more I nurture you to grow,
> the more the fruits of my labor
> will show. Money tree, bring to
> me the abundance my
> mind's eye can see.

Place the green calcite crystal on top of the soil to enhance your tree's money and prosperity power. Once a week, light green candles around the pot and repeat the above incantation. Water and fertilize your tree regularly, and make sure it gets plenty of light. (The ideal place would be at the entrance of your front or back door.)

Spell for a Harmonious Work Environment

Time:

🌀 Perform this spell on a Monday or Wednesday, when the moon is waning.

last

You Will Need:

🌀 1 quart water

🌀 1 Tbsp. fresh basil

🌀 1 Tbsp. frankincense

🌀 1 tsp. vervain

🌀 1 tsp. valerian

🌀 1 saucepan

🌀 1 ceramic bowl

🌀 A wand or wooden spoon

🌀 A desire to bring balance and harmony into your relationships

Action:

Place the herbs and water in the saucepan, and heat over a low flame. When the potion begins to simmer, stir it in a clockwise direction with your wand or wooden spoon. Invoke the goddess Brigit and imagine her nurturing, compassionate spirit infusing the potion with love. Say,

Gracious goddess of the hearth,
charge this potion with the power
to create harmonious work relations.
Protect us from negative energy,
and open our hearts and minds to
the joy of creative inspiration.

Pour the potion into the bowl and let it cool. When you're alone at work, place the candles and incense in each corner of the building and light them. Then, in a clockwise direction, sprinkle the potion on the floor in every room, or if it's a huge company, in the area you work in. You can now look forward to a happy and productive work environment.

Spell to Speed Up Promotion

Time:

⑨ Perform this spell on a Tuesday, when the moon is waxing.

First

You Will Need:

⑨ 1 green candle

⑨ A pentacle (made from any material)

⑨ Ambition, desire, and a strong sense of self-worth

Action:

Light the candle and sit down in the center of your circle. Take the pentacle in your right hand and charge it with your energy—instruct it to be your manifestation talisman. Then close your eyes and concentrate on your goal. Feel your strength and confidence, and visualize your promotion. See your efforts bringing recognition and opportunity to you. Then call upon the powers of Merlin to help you attain your goal:

All-powerful Merlin, great master of magic,
Ensure that the attainment of my goal is quick.
So be it.

Now snuff out the candle and put the pentacle in your pocket. Keep it with you at all times. You will now move more easily to victory.

Spell to Inspire Quick Payment

Time:

🌀 Perform this spell on a Wednesday or Thursday, when the moon is nearly full.

You Will Need:

🌀 1 green candle

🌀 1 purple candle

🌀 Money Oil:
>   3 Tbsp. jojoba oil
>   2 drops orange oil
>   2 drops bergamot oil
>   2 drops sandalwood oil

🌀 Frankincense incense

🌀 A determination to succeed

Action:

Light the incense, and anoint the candles with money oil. Then empower the candles with your energy as they burn. With the green candle in your right hand and the purple candle in your left hand, say,

I charge these candles to bring me . . .
[state how much money you want].
Money, money, come to me.

Now close your eyes and call upon Vishnu to help activate your spell. Visualize his light and warmth, and see the person who owes you money succumbing to your powers of persuasion. For several minutes, picture him or her writing you a check or depositing the money in your bank account. Within a few days, your wish will be granted.

ⓢ ⓢ ⓢ

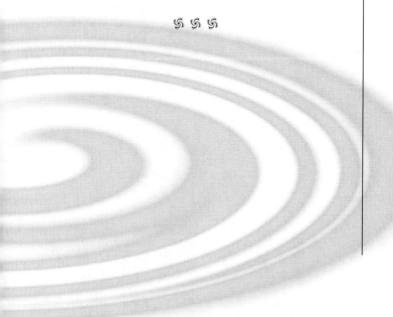

CHAPTER FOURTEEN

Healing and Protection

Spell to End
Negative Thinking

Time:

ⓢ Perform this spell on a Saturday,
when the moon is waning. *Last*

You Will Need:

ⓢ 4 black candles
ⓢ 1 black pen
ⓢ 1 piece of paper

ᔕ 1 metal sieve

ᔕ Endurance and perseverance

ᔕ Faith in your own destiny

Action:

Place the candles at the four cardinal points of your circle (north, south, east, and west), and light them. Then charge the crystal with your energy while reflecting on your current state of mind. Does nothing in your life seem to go right? It may be that your life lacks direction because of financial burdens, or because every man/woman you go out with is a loser. Whatever the reason, it's important to recognize that dark thoughts destroy inner clarity and create a pattern of negative events in your life. This spell will help you break the cycle. On the piece of paper, make a list in black ink of all the doubts, fears, and problems that cloud your insight. At the end of the list, write,

A cycle of adversity has come to an end.
My doubts and fears no longer
bend my beliefs about reality.
Now that I have fought my fight,
I know which path in life is right.
So be it.

Read the affirmation out loud with conviction, then tear the list into tiny pieces. Place the paper and crystal in the metal sieve and wave it over the candle flame in front of you. As the paper burns to ash, discard any doubts or fears—they no longer have any effect on you. Picture what your future will be like, unproblematic and happy, and see yourself attain that which you long for. Release the ash into the wind, and keep the crystal as a symbol of your new trust in life.

Spell to Restore
Your Energy

Time:

§ Perform this spell on a Tuesday or Sunday, when the moon is new, waxing, or full.

First

You Will Need:

§ 3 Tbsp. fresh rosemary

§ Rosewood oil

§ A desire to rejuvenate your neglected self

Action:

Prepare some rosemary tea, and go outdoors to a sacred spot or to a quiet place in your garden. Facing the sun, cast a circle and sit calmly within it with your ingredients in front of you. Anoint your wrists and third eye with rosewood oil (which is great for restoring energy), then briefly consider the areas of your life that drain and deplete you. Vow to correct these imbalances and make more time for yourself. Close your eyes and bask in the renewed harmony that the sun's energy brings. Feel your skin, hot and alive, and allow your mind to dissolve in pleasure. When you're ready, invoke and honor the sun god Ra:

> *Gracious Ra, great god of the sun,*
> *Your energy infuses me*
> *with new life and vitality.*
> *May my energy grow*
> *from this moment.*

Continue to absorb the sun's light and warmth as you drink the tea. When you've finished your tea, close the circle. Eat well, get plenty of sleep, and repeat this spell once a week for three weeks. You will soon notice a vast improvement in your energy level.

Spell to Cure a Headache

Time:

🌀 Perform this spell whenever your head aches, but ideally when the moon is waning.

You Will Need:

🌀 3 drops lavender oil

🌀 2 Tbsp. sweet marjoram

🌀 1 square of muslin (8" x 8")

🌀 1 blue ribbon (8")

🌀 1 blue candle

🌀 2 small hematite crystals

🌀 A desire to dispel your stress-related headache

Action:

Place the marjoram in the middle of the muslin and tie it up with ribbon. Run yourself a warm bath, and hang the muslin bag from the tap so the water gushes through it. Add the oil to the bathwater when it's full, and light the candle at the end of the tub. Climb in and relax. Breathe in the healing vapors of the lavender and sweet marjoram—calming, soothing, and balancing.

Now, for 15 minutes, close your eyes, and with the hematite crystals, firmly massage the pressure points on either side of your vertebral column at the base of your skull. Feel the pain and tension drain from your head into the hematite, and imagine yourself being headache free. When the pain has lifted, blow out the candle, and say, "Headache begone." Your discomfort should not return.

Spell to Let Go of the Past

Time:

🕉 Perform this spell on a Saturday, when the moon is waning.

You Will Need:

🕉 1 black ribbon (1 yard)

🕉 1 piece of paper

🕉 1 black pen

🕉 1 tsp. frankincense and myrrh

🕉 1 charcoal disk

🕉 1 metal incense burner

🕉 A pair of scissors

🕉 An object that represents an aspect of your past that you wish to let go of— it may be a photo, a piece of jewelry, or some other symbol

🕉 A desire to move on in life

Action:

Assemble the spell ingredients and cast a circle. Light the charcoal disk and place it on the incense burner. When the charcoal is red-hot, sprinkle on the frankincense and myrrh. Then, on the piece of paper, write:

> *I neutralize the power of my past*
> *so it cannot affect my life in the*
> *present moment or in the future.*
> *So be it.*

Roll up the object that represents your past in the piece of paper and attach it to one end of the ribbon, knotting it several times. Then attach the other end of the ribbon to your left arm. Spend a few minutes thinking about the old ways that have become limiting, preventing you from moving on in your life. When you're clear about the relationships, feelings, or patterns of behavior you wish to abandon, cut the ribbon. This act of letting go will liberate you.

Spell to Banish Bad Vibes

Time:

§ Perform this spell at dusk on a Monday or Thursday, when the moon is waning.

You Will Need:

§ 3 sticks of frankincense incense

§ 3 Tbsp. vervain

§ 3 Tbsp. rosemary

§ 3 Tbsp. frankincense and myrrh

§ 3 Tbsp. salt

§ 3 lemons

§ 3 cloves of garlic

§ 3 quarts of water

§ 6 drops lavender oil

§ 1 large saucepan

§ 1 wand or wooden spoon

ⓢ A black candle for every room of
the house

ⓢ A small bowl for every room of
the house

Action:

Close all the windows and doors of your
house, and light a black candle in every
room. Fill the saucepan with water and bring
it to boil. Juice the lemons, chop the garlic,
grind the herbs to a powder, and place them
all in the saucepan. Then add the salt and
lavender oil, and brew for ten minutes. When
the potion is ready, pour half of it into the
bowls, and place one bowl in each room. Use
the rest of the mixture to wash any areas of
your house that particularly need cleansing.
You might like to clean the bathroom and/or
kitchen floor, or perhaps the doorways and
entrance to your home. Now, light the
incense and walk with it through every
room, circling it in a clockwise direction,
saying,

As I *cleanse and purify this room,*
I *repel bad energy that may loom.*
Evil spirits cannot dwell wherever
I *cast my powerful spell.*
Negativity begone.

When you've finished, snuff out the candles. After three hours, remove the potion from each room and empty it in the garden.

Spell for a Safe Journey

Time:

🕉 Perform this spell on a Wednesday, when the moon is new.

You Will Need:

🕉 A length of thin leather cord (2⅓ ft.)

🕉 1 turquoise amulet

🕉 1 red candle

🕉 1 red ribbon (8")

🕉 1 sprig of rosemary

🕉 1 Tbsp. salt

🕉 1 bowl of water

🕉 Courage, and the knowledge that you're protected when you venture into the unknown

Action:

Mix the salt into the bowl of water, and add the turquoise amulet. At dawn, place the bowl outside where it can get plenty of sunlight to cleanse and charge the stone. At dusk, assemble your ingredients and cast a circle. Light the candle, hold the turquoise amulet in your right hand, and visualize a perfect journey. See yourself traveling with ease on your journey, moving over obstacles and through fear, and know that you'll exude such an openness and warmth that like-minded people will be drawn to you as if by a magnet. When you're ready, thread the turquoise amulet onto the leather cord and bind it to the sprig of rosemary with ribbon. Knot the ribbon four times, saying, "I knot this ribbon to protect against harm." Then snuff out the candle and close the circle. Sleep with the amulet, cord, and rosemary under your pillow until your day of departure. Just before you're about to leave, untie the ribbon, remove the rosemary, and tie the amulet around your neck or wrist. It will protect you against harm during your travels, and bring you many friends.

Spell for Self-Empowerment

Time:

🌀 Perform this spell on Friday, when the moon is full. ⟨May 16⟩

You Will Need:

🌀 2 red candles

🌀 1 white candle

🌀 4 drops jasmine oil

🌀 2 drops patchouli oil

🌀 3 drops sandalwood oil

🌀 A glass of champagne

🌀 A full-length mirror

Action:

Run yourself a warm bath, add the oils, and bathe in the light of the red candles. Make sure the atmosphere is tranquil and quiet, and allow your mind to be filled with thoughts of eternal hope for the future. Know that no incident, person, or problem can stand in the way of your destiny, and that every setback you've experienced until now has only served to intensify your power. When you've finished, dry yourself off with a clean towel and pour yourself a glass of champagne. Then stand in front of the mirror by the light of the white candle. For several minutes, observe your body without judgment. Don't see yourself as sexy or ugly; just admire what an incredible work of creation you are—unique, strong, and beautiful. Cast a circle of salt around yourself, and imagine that a protective beam of white light surrounds your body. Now invoke and honor the goddess Diana:

Goddess of the hunt, goddess of the moon,
Your freedom and strength imbue me with light.
Protect and empower me by day and by night.
So be it.

Toast yourself with the champagne, then snuff out the candle and close the circle. If you like, you can reinforce the power of your spell by taking a walk in the moonlight. Look up at the moon and feel your magic working.

ரு ரு ரு

AFTERWORD

Make Your Own Magic

The best spells are those that you develop yourself. Hopefully the spells in this book have inspired you to create your own. Many of the rituals and practices I mentioned are based on ancient traditions, and they provide an effective framework for working successful magic. However, I'm not suggesting that you should adhere to tradition for its own sake. The idea is to follow your instincts and do what feels right for you, as it's your power that determines a spell's success.

§ § §

❦ Bibliography ❦

Black, Greaves, Sterling, *Astrology Under the Southern Cross*. NSW, Australia: Random House, 1998.

Bradley, M. Z. *The Mists of Avalon*. New York: Ballantine Books, 1982.

Cabot, L. & Cowan, T. *Love Magic*. London: Pan Books, 1994.

——. *Power of the Witch*. London: Penguin Books, 1992.

Cunningham, S. *Cunningham's Encyclopedia of Crystal, Gem and Metal Magic*. St. Paul, Minnesota: Llewellyn Publications, 1994.

Drury, N. *The History of Magic in the Modern Age*. NSW, Australia: Simon and Schuster, 2000.

Elizabeth, E. *A Recipe Book of Spells*. NSW, Australia: Sandstone Publishing, 1999.

Estes, Clarissa P. *Women Who Run with the Wolves*. New York: Ballantine Books, 1995 (reprint).

Farrar, J. & S. *The Witches' Goddess*. Blaine, Washington: Phoenix Publishing, 1987.

Gonzalez-Wippler, M. *The Complete Book of Spells, Ceremonies and Magic*. St. Paul, Minnesota: Llewellyn Publications, 1996.

Green, M. *Spells*. NSW, Australia: Lansdowne, 1997.

Horne, F. Witch: *A Magickal Year*. NSW, Australia: Random House, 1999.

McArthur Margie, *Wisdom of the Elements*. Santa Cruz, California: The Crossing Press, 1998.

Telesco, P. *The Urban Pagan*. St. Paul, Minnesota: Llewellyn Publications, 1995.

Valiente, D. *An ABC of Witchcraft*. Blaine, Washington: Phoenix Publishing, 1973.

Warner, R. (Fwd) *Encyclopedia of World Mythology*. London: Peerage Books, 1975.

Ⓢ Ⓢ Ⓢ

About the Author

Claudia Blaxell is a researcher, writer, and author. For the past seven years, she has specialized in the fields of alternative spirituality and modern esoteric thought. Claudia lives in Sydney, Australia, where she freelances. This is her first book.

෧ ෧ ෧

july 10 | page (85)
11   18 | 65
11   08 | 98
May 24 ─────── 103

june 23 | page
        | 112

§ Notes

Notes